Health
wellbeing
£3

B
6/23

D1379953

Law of
ATTRACTION

Michael J. Losier

**HODDER
MOBIUS**

First published in Great Britain in 2007 by Hodder & Stoughton
A division of Hodder Headline

The right of Michael J. Losier to be identified as the Author of the
Work has been asserted by him in accordance with the Copyright,
Designs and Patents Act 1988.

A Mobius Book

1

A CIP catalogue record for this title is available from the British Library

Hardback ISBN 978 0 340 95333 4
Paperback ISBN 978 0 340 95352 5

Printed and bound by Mackays of Chatham Ltd, Chatham, Kent.

Hodder Headline's policy is to use papers that are natural, renewable
and recyclable products and made from wood grown in sustainable
forests. The logging and manufacturing processes are expected to
conform to the environmental regulations of the country of origin.

Hodder & Stoughton Ltd
A division of Hodder Headline
338 Euston Road
London NW1 3BH

Table of Contents

What Others Are Saying About This Book

"Michael Losier's message will change the way you view yourself and others. I found Law of Attraction *both inspiring and healing."*

> Ethelle G. Lord, M.Ed., CCG
> Teamwork Development Associates
> www.teamworkcoaching.com

"Michael Losier has a gift for being able to distill abstract principles into results that work. Law of Attraction *is easy to read, easy to apply, and best of all, it really works!"*

> Mary Marcdante, Speaker,
> Author of *My Mother, My Friend*
> www.marymarcdante.com

"If you want to really understand why your life is the way it is and if you really want to know how you can change it to anything you want, here is the instruction book, and it is in plain language."

> Mark Foster, Wigan UK

"I've read other Law of Attraction books but something seemed to be missing. Losier provides the missing piece through his Clarity Through Contrast and Desire Statement worksheets."

> Janet Boyer, New Age Editor
> www.NewAgeBellaOnline.com

"What an outstanding book! Michael's short and simple formula for attracting anything your heart desires will work big time for he or she that follows it. I highly recommend you apply his principles in your life to achieve mega success!"

> Zev Saftlas, Author of *Motivation That Works*
> and founder of www.EmpoweringMessages.com

"This book supports the proposition that simplicity is the best design. Short and simple, the author provides a good working outline of the principles underlying the Law of Attraction and then provides practical exercises to assist the reader in utilizing them."

Antigone W., Amazon.com Reader

"You may have heard about the Law of Attraction and read about it before. Michael takes the understanding of the Law of Attraction and presents it crisply and simply, in a way that anyone can hear it and understand it, from someone brand new to the Law of Attraction to the most experienced. An easy, delightful read!"

Eva Gregory, Amazon.com Reader
Author of *The Feel Good Guide to Prosperity*

"Totally by chance, I was extremely fortunate to see Michael Losier present his "Law of Attraction" seminar. Michael is an entertaining, dynamic, and honest speaker, and his teachings have changed my life. As an upbeat and positive person, I was extremely surprised to learn how much of my daily self-talk was actually sabotaging my efforts to attract the type of relationships and things I wanted in life (and I've read hundreds of other personal development books by today's top gurus). Michael's methods are far more than positive affirmations or fluffy new age mantras. His material is practical, easily learned, and although deceptively simple, it is extremely powerful. The Law of Attraction *book is a great value, and I highly recommend it to anyone who is interested in increasing his or her quality of life."*

John Goudie, Youth at Risk Counsellor

"Out of all the books, tapes, and resources that I've purchased on the topic of "creating your ideal life," Michael Losier's Law of Attraction *is the absolute best "nuts-and-bolts" treatment I've ever read. Period. What Losier teaches in this book is NOT how to become someone who attracts results – you're already doing that. Instead, he teaches you, in plain English with no weird jargon, how to become a DELIBERATE attractor and start consciously attracting more of the things you want out of life and less of the things that you don't want. This book has my highest recommendation. If I couldn't get another copy, I wouldn't take $1,000 for mine."*

Tony Rush, Life Coach, Alabama

A Brief History of the Law of Attraction

Some of you have heard reference to the Law of Attraction from various sources while others are just beginning to learn about it. In modern times the Law of Attraction has been documented since the early 1900s. Here's a brief history:

1906 - Atkinson, William Walter
Thought Vibration or the Law of Attraction in the Thought World

1926 - Holmes, Ernest
Basic Ideas of Science of Mind

1949 - Holliwell, Dr. Raymond
Working with the Law

In the early 1990s, information and teachings on the Law of Attraction became widely available through the publications of Jerry and Esther Hicks. (Refer to their website for all current teachings/papers – www.abraham-hicks.com.) It is through their teachings that I really "got it."

Since 2000, many articles and books have been written about the Law of Attraction, and its appeal has expanded to a much broader audience. The future holds many more authors and teachers writing on this topic as the message of the Law of Attraction continues to grow in its mass appeal.

What Makes This Book Different?

In 1995 I studied NLP (Neuro Linguistic Programming) to understand how our mind and thoughts work. This led me to many insights on how people learn. You'll notice while reading this book that it appeals to your and others' reading style. This book is written in such a way that each section builds on the last and as in any training manual, you can use the tools, exercises and scripts to keep you connected to the Law of Attraction.

Many of the books I've studied were broad in their theoretical approach to the subject of the Law of Attraction. Nowhere could I find an answer to my question, "How do I actually DO this?" With my knowledge of NLP and how to teach using different learning styles, I created an easy-to-follow HOW-TO book for students of the Law of Attraction. Using the exercises and tools in this book, you will be able to learn quickly so you can begin practicing the Law of Attraction in your own life.

The most frequent and satisfying compliment I receive is that my book is SIMPLE to read and the exercises are easy to follow. This book has been embraced by a multitude of different religious and spiritual groups. In addition, it has become required reading for many sales groups, network marketing companies, realtors, financial advisors and other business organizations. In short, this book has mass appeal.

You're Already Experiencing the Law of Attraction

Have you noticed that sometimes what you need just falls into place or comes to you from an out-of-the-blue telephone call? Or you've bumped into someone on the street you've been thinking about? Perhaps you've met the perfect client or life partner, just by fate or being at the right place at the right time. All of these experiences are evidence of the Law of Attraction in your life.

Have you heard about people who find themselves in bad relationships over and over again, and who are always complaining that they keep attracting the same kind of relationship? The Law of Attraction is at work for them too.

The Law of Attraction may be defined as: *I attract to my life whatever I give my attention, energy and focus to, whether positive or negative.* By reading this book you'll come to understand why and how this happens.

There are a number of words or expressions that describe evidence of the Law of Attraction. If you've ever used any of these words or expressions you're actually referring to the Law of Attraction.

Here are just a few:

◆ Out-of-the-blue
◆ Serendipity
◆ Coincidence
◆ Fate
◆ Karma
◆ Fell into place
◆ Synchronicity
◆ Luck
◆ Meant to be

In this book you'll learn why these experiences happen. More importantly, you'll discover how you can use the Law of Attraction more deliberately. You'll be able to attract all that you need to do, know and have, so you can get more of what you want and less of what you don't want. As a result, you'll have your ideal client, your ideal job, your ideal relationship, your ideal vacation, your ideal health, more money in your life, and all that you desire. Really!

The Science of the Law of Attraction

There is a physiological foundation for positive thinking and its effect in creating the Law of Attraction.

There are many forms of energy: atomic, thermal, electromotive, kinetic and potential. Energy can never be destroyed.

You may also recall that all matter is made up of atoms, and that each atom has a nucleus (containing protons and neutrons), around which orbit electrons.

Electrons in atoms always orbit the nucleus in prescribed "orbitals" or energy levels that assure the stability of the atom. Electrons may be compelled to assume "higher" orbits by the addition of energy, or may give off energy when they drop to a "lower" orbit. When it comes to "vibrations," if atoms are "aligned," they create a motive force, all pulling together in the same direction in much the same way as metals can be magnetized by aligning their molecules in the same direction. This creation of positive (+) and negative (–) poles is a fact of nature and science. Suffice to say, science has shown that if there are physical laws that can be observed and quantified in one arena, there are most probably similar laws in other arenas, even if they cannot be quantified at this time.

So you see, the Law of Attraction isn't a fancy term or new-age magic. It is a law of nature that every atom of your being is in constant response to, whether you know it or not.

For readers who want to find out more about the connection between energy, our thoughts and the world of 'matter' around us, I recommend watching the movie, What the Bleep Do We Know © 2004 Captured Light & Lord of the Wind Films, LLC.

Making Reference to the Law of Attraction

Many authors have written about the Law of Attraction. Here are just a few of the many ways the Law of Attraction has been referred to in various books.

That which is like unto itself is drawn.
> Jerry and Esther Hicks, *(The Teachings of Abraham) Ask and It Is Given*

What you radiate outward in your thoughts, feelings, mental pictures and words, you attract into you life.
> Catherine Ponder, *Dynamic Law of Prosperity*

Never expect a thing you do not want, and never desire a thing you do not expect. When you expect something you do not want, you attract the undesirable, and when you desire a thing that is not expected, you simply dissipate valuable mental force. On the other hand, when you constantly expect that which you persistently desire, your ability to attract becomes irresistible. The mind is a magnet and attracts whatever corresponds to its ruling state.
> Dr. Raymond Holliwell, *Working with the Law 11 Truth Principles for Successful Living*

Every thought must manifest according to its intensity. The slightest thought of Intelligence sets in motion a power in the Law to produce a corresponding thing.
> Ernst Holmes, *Basic Ideas of Science of Mind*

You are a living magnet; you attract into your life people, situations and circumstances that are in harmony with your dominant thoughts. Whatever you dwell on in the conscious grows in your experience.
> Brian Tracy

Positive and Negative Vibrations

Definition of the Law of Attraction

I attract to my life whatever I give my attention, energy and focus to, whether positive or negative.

Positive and Negative Vibrations

The word *vibe* is often used to describe a mood or a feeling that you pick up from someone or something. For example, you may say you pick up a *good vibe* when you are around a certain person. Or you may say that you get a *negative vibe* when you walk in a certain part of a city or neighbourhood. In all of these cases, the word *vibe* is used to describe the mood or feeling you are experiencing. In short, a *vibe* equals a mood or a feeling.

The word *vibe* comes from the longer word vibration (which isn't used often by most people). In the 'vibrational' world, there are only two kinds of vibrations, positive (+) and negative (−). Every mood or feeling causes you to emit, send-out or offer a vibration, whether positive or negative. If you go through the dictionary and select every word that describes a feeling, you would be able to put them into either of these two categories. Each word will describe a feeling that generates a positive vibration or describe a feeling that generates a negative vibration.

Each one of us sends out either a positive or negative vibration. In fact, we are always sending a vibration. Think about the expression "He gives off good vibes," or "This neighbourhood gives me negative vibes."

On the following page you'll see examples of feelings that generate positive or negative vibrations.

Vibrations (feelings)

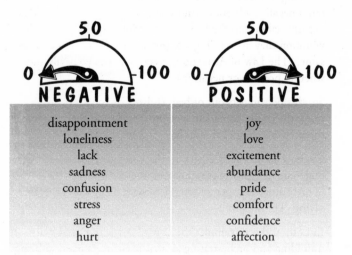

NEGATIVE	POSITIVE
disappointment	joy
loneliness	love
lack	excitement
sadness	abundance
confusion	pride
stress	comfort
anger	confidence
hurt	affection

Every single moment you have a mood or a feeling. In this moment right now, the mood or feeling you are experiencing is causing you to emit or send out a negative or positive vibration.

Here's where the Law of Attraction comes in. The Law of Attraction (universal energy around you that obeys the science of physics) is responding to the vibration you are offering. Right now, in this very moment, it is matching your vibration by giving you more of the same, whether positive or negative.

For example, when a person wakes up first thing Monday morning feeling a little bit cranky and irritated, they are sending out a negative vibration. And while they are sending out this negative vibration, the Law of Attraction responds, matching the vibration they are sending and giving this person more of the same. (The Law of Attraction always matches your vibration – whether positive or negative.)

So, this person gets out of bed, stubs their toe, burns their toast, the traffic is snarled, a client cancels and then they catch themselves saying "I should have stayed in bed!"

Or, how about the salesperson who is joyfully excited about a huge sale they just made, thus sending out a positive vibration. Shortly after, they get another ideal sale. They catch themselves saying "I'm on a roll!"

In both of these examples the Law of Attraction is at work, unfolding and orchestrating all that needs to happen to bring them more of the same, whether positive or negative.

In this book you will learn how to identify the vibration you are sending and be able to make a conscious choice whether you want to keep sending it or change it. In the Deliberate Attraction section of this book you will learn what to do to deliberately send a different vibration. You will learn how to become a deliberate 'sender' of your vibration so that you can change the results you've been getting and have more of what you do want and less of what you don't.

The Law of Attraction responds to whatever vibration you are sending by giving you more of it, whether it's positive or negative. It simply responds to your vibration.

Non-deliberate Attraction

Many people are often curious about why they keep attracting the same thing over and over again. They are absolutely certain that they are not sending out anything negative, yet in a specific area of their life, negative experiences keep showing up. This happens because they are sending a negative vibe non-deliberately simply through their observation of what they are currently getting.

For example, if you open your wallet and don't see any money, by observing that you're not seeing any money there, you are now offering a vibration of lack, fear or some other similar negative vibration. Although you're not doing it on purpose, the Law of Attraction is simply responding to your vibration and giving you more of the same. It doesn't know what action you are taking that is causing you to generate this negative vibration. You might be remembering, or pretending, or daydreaming, or in this case just merely observing.

Observation Cycle
(Non-deliberate Attraction)

1 You observe what you receive and have in your life (whether positve or negative).

2 While observing, you are sending a vibration, either negative or positive.

3 The Law of Attraction responds to the vibration you are sending.

4 As a result, you get more of what you were vibrating, whether positive or negative.

As you observe what you are receiving in different areas of your life (money, work, health, relationships, etc.), your observations generate a feeling (vibration) that can be either positive or negative.

Observing Sends a Vibration

Even though you may not be aware of it, you are perpetuating the Observation Cycle. The Law of Attraction will respond to your vibration, whether positive or negative, by giving you more of what you are vibrating.

It's important to understand that the Law of Attraction is already existing in your life whether you understand it or not, whether you like it or not, or whether you believe it or not. If you like what you are observing, then celebrate it, and in your celebration you will more of it. If you don't like what you are getting, then it is time to tap into the Law of Attraction more deliberately so you can stop attracting what you don't want and start attracting what you do. In other words – Deliberate Attraction.

Whether it's a positive or negative vibration, the Law of Attraction will give you more of the same.

Understanding the Significance of Your Words

Words, Words, Words

Most of the tools and worksheets in this book are related to language, the use of words, and more importantly, the feelings generated by words.

As you read on in this book you'll learn how words are the common denominator for all of the exercises in the Deliberate Attraction process.

Why Is There Such an Emphasis on Words?

Words are everywhere. We speak them, read them, write them, think them, see them, type them, and hear them in our head. The reason the exercises in this book are all based on choosing precise words is because the words we think and use generate the vibration we send out. The word 'homework', for example, can cause some people to have a negative vibration and others to have a positive vibration. The word 'money' can hold a positive vibration for some people and a negative vibration for others. In the following pages you'll learn which words are causing you to attract the things you don't want.

Your thoughts are made up of words. Here is an illustration showing the connection between positive and negative vibrations, your thoughts, and your words.

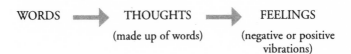

WORDS ➡ THOUGHTS ➡ FEELINGS
(made up of words) (negative or positive vibrations)

Words That Are Causing You to Attract What You DON'T Want

Don't, Not and No

Don't think of the Statue of Liberty in New York. I know that you just did! Your unconscious and conscious mind automatically filters out the words **don't**, **not** and **no**. When you use these words you are actually internalizing in your mind the exact thing you are being told *not* to. For example, if I said "Do not think of a snowstorm," I guarantee you would start thinking of a snowstorm almost immediately. Even though the instruction was *not* to do something, your unconscious and conscious mind edited out that part of the instruction.

There are other common expressions that give more attention and energy to what you DON'T want. Have you heard yourself use any of these statements?

Don't get mad	Don't panic
I'm not blaming	No rush, no worry
Don't hesitate to call me	Don't look now
Don't be fooled	Don't run with scissors
Don't worry	Don't forget
I don't want this to hurt	I don't want my clients
Don't litter	to cancel
Don't smoke	Don't be late
I'm not judging	Don't slam the door

The Law of Attraction responds the same way your mind does: it hears what you DON'T want. When you hear yourself make a statement containing the words **don't**, **not** or **no**, you are actually giving attention and energy to what you DON'T want.

Here's an effective and easy tool that will help you reduce and eventually eliminate the use of the words **don't**, **not** and **no** from your vocabulary. Each time you hear yourself using **don't**, **not** or **no**, ask yourself "So, what do I want?" Each time you talk about what you DON'T want, in that moment you are giving it your attention and energy. When you ask yourself what you DO want, the answer will have created a new sentence with new words. When your words change, your vibration changes, and the best news of all is that you can only send out one vibration at a time.

When you make a statement containing the words don't, not or no, you are actually giving attention and energy to what you don't want.

Simply ask yourself "SO, WHAT DO I WANT?"

Asking yourself, "So, what do I want?"

When we use *don't, not* and *no,* here's how the new sentences will sound after you've asked yourself "So, what do I want?"

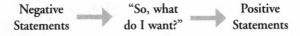

Negative Statements	"So, what do I want?"	Positive Statements

Negative Statements	Positive Statements
Don't hesitate to call	Call me soon
Don't panic	Stay calm
Don't forget	Remember to…
Don't be late	See you on time
Don't slam the door	Close it quietly
I don't want this to hurt	I'll be fine
I don't want my clients to cancel	I want my clients to keep their appointments
When do *you* use **don't, not** and **no**? Add your own sentences here.	Create new positive sentences here.
◆	◆
◆	◆
◆	◆
◆	◆
◆	

"Positive and negative emotions cannot occupy the mind at the same time. One or the other must dominate. It is your responsibility to make sure that positive emotions constitute the dominating influence of your mind."

Napolean Hill

When you go from what you don't want to what you do want, the words change. When the words change, the vibration changes, and you can only send out one vibration at a time.

Resetting Your Vibration

At every moment you can tell if the vibration you are sending is either positive or negative by identifying the feeling you are experiencing. These feelings are causing you to send out a vibration, and in the 'vibrational' world there are only two kinds of vibrations: positive and negative.

You can reset your vibration from negative to positive by simply choosing different words and different thoughts. It's as easy as asking yourself "So, what do I want?" Again, when you talk about what you don't want and then talk about what you do want, the words change. You can only send out one vibration at a time, thus

when your words change, your vibration changes too. Simply put, to reset your vibration, just change the words you're using and the thoughts you are thinking.

The Law of Attraction doesn't remember what vibration you were sending out five minutes ago, five days ago, five months ago or 50 years ago. It's only responding to the vibration you are sending out right now in this very moment and giving you more of the same.

To know whether you are sending out a positive or negative vibration, simply take a look at the results you're getting in that area of your life. They are a perfect reflection of what you are vibrating.

Deliberate Attraction

In the next section you are going to discover how to use the Law of Attraction more **deliberately**. To do this, you'll learn an easy 3-step formula. In addition to learning the steps and following along with two case studies, you can participate by filling in the blank worksheets I have provided. More worksheets are available at www.LawofAttractionBook.com/worksheets.html

If you are not sure what specific area of your life you'd like to apply Deliberate Attraction to, simply choose the area that you feel the least satisfied with. It could be your relationship(s), career, health, business or your financial situation.

I recommend you finish reading the remainder of this book and then go back and do the exercises, applying them to the specific area you've chosen.

The 3-Step Formula
for Deliberate Attraction

Step 1: Identify Your Desire

Sounds easy, right? Most people are not very good at knowing what they do want, however, they are very good at identifying what they don't want. In this step you'll learn why knowing what you *don't* like is helpful.

Step 2: Give Your Desire Attention

The Law of Attraction will give you more of what you give your attention, energy and focus to. This step will teach you how to do just that, simply by learning how to choose *your words*.

Step 3: Allow It

Wondering why you're not manifesting your desires? The speed at which your desires come to you depends on how much you're Allowing. This is the most important step.

3
STEPS

Identify Your Desire

Give Your Desire Attention

Allow It

Step 1 - Identify Your Desire

The first step in making the Law of Attraction work for you
is to be clear about what you want. The challenge, however,
is that most people are not good at knowing what they DO
want but they are good at identifying what they DON'T want.
Knowing what you don't want is actually good news. As you'll
discover in this section, knowing what you don't want will
become a helpful tool for you.

What is Contrast?

Contrast*, as it applies to the Law of Attraction, is anything you
don't like, doesn't feel good, or causes you to be in a negative
mood. The moment you identify something in your life that feels
like contrast and you spend time complaining about it, talking
about it, or declaring that you don't want it, you are offering a
negative vibration. The Law of Attraction then responds to your
negative vibration by giving you more of the same.

Is Contrast Helpful?

Yes. By observing contrast and identifying it as something you
don't want, you become clearer about what you do want. Simply
ask yourself "So, what do I want?" In other words, you can use
the contrast to gain clarity about what you do want by answering
that question.

Take your first boyfriend or girlfriend, for example. Chances
are you're no longer with that person and from that relationship
you have a list of things that you didn't like. This is your list of
contrast. It is this list that will help you become clear about what
you do want in a partner.

* The concept of "contrast" is a distinction I learned from Jerry and Esther
  Hicks, Abraham-Hicks Publications.

Observing contrast is essential because it helps you to become clearer about what you do want.

Why Is It Important to Identify Contrast?

You are already experiencing clarity whenever you observe contrast in your life.

Imagine you are riding in your car with your best friend who insists on fiddling with the radio dial. Your friend chooses a heavy metal station that you hate. You begin to feel stressed.

After five seconds of the music you say to yourself "This is my car and I'm not listening to this for one second longer." You reach over and change the dial to your favorite station, which plays adult contemporary music. Instantly, you feel happier and more relaxed.

Notice how you become clear about what you like by paying attention to what you don't like? In other words, your contrast has provided you with clarity.

To help you observe contrast briefly, say, "So, what do I want?"

How Long Is Briefly?

The key to getting what you want without getting stuck focusing on what you don't want is to briefly observe contrast.

Only you can decide how long *briefly* is. For some, experiencing contrast in a relationship may last for years; for others, contrast is observed for a short time. You might decide to end a relationship on the first date.

Notice that when you experience contrast around smells, sounds, or tastes, your tolerance is minimal. Think about these statements:

How long would you smell something that doesn't smell good?
How long would you listen to music that doesn't sound good?
How long would you eat something that doesn't taste good?

In these cases, you are observing contrast briefly and changing it to clarity, FAST.

There are, however, a few areas of your life where you may observe contrast far too long:

◆ Relationships ◆ Career
◆ Health ◆ Other
◆ Money

Generally, the least amount of time you spend putting your attention, energy and focus toward contrast, the better. The Clarity Through Contrast process, which you'll learn from this book, will help you with this.

Identify what makes you feel good and do more of it.

Your Goal is to Limit Contrast in All Areas of Your Life

It's OK to feel good in all areas of your life. Does this sound selfish? It's OK to be selfish when you understand that being selfish is simply an act of self-care.

Selfish = Self-Care

- Are you selfish about what you eat?
- Are you selfish about what you smell?
- Are you selfish about what you wear?
- Are you selfish about what you listen to?

I'm encouraging you to be selfish in all areas of your life, especially in your:

- Career
- Finances
- Health
- Relationship

In these four areas people tend to have lots of negative emotions and observe them for a long time, in many cases, years.

The Clarity Through Contrast Process

The Clarity Through Contrast process will assist you in becoming clearer about your desires.

Here are some prominent areas in your life where clarity is beneficial:

◆ Career
◆ Money
◆ Life partner relationships
◆ Friendships
◆ Work relationships
◆ Business clients
◆ Business referrals
◆ Education
◆ Health
◆ Other

Next we'll examine two case studies that illustrate how the Clarity Through Contrast Process helped generate clarity.

Case Studies

After teaching the Law of Attraction to thousands of students, I've collected wonderful stories about people whose lives have been changed working with this process. There's something about seeing someone else's story in print that really makes this tool come alive, so I've included two case studies that represent two common areas where people use the Law of Attraction to get more of what they want.

Janice's story will show you how the 3 steps, Identifying Your Desire, Giving it Attention, and Allowing can work in attracting an ideal relationship. Greg's story focuses on another difficult issue for many people – money.

Janice - Relationships

Janice, 34, is tired and frustrated because she continually has the wrong kind of guy showing interest in her. She complains that she attracts men who are unavailable, insensitive, and who seldom make her a priority.

Janice decided to use the Law of Attraction to attract her ideal relationship.

She began the process of Deliberate Attraction with Step One, Identify Your Desire, using the Clarity Through Contrast Worksheet. Take a look at Janice's worksheet on the next page.

In Janice's case, she was able to build a large list of contrast by recalling a number of past relationships, and what she didn't like (contrast) about those relationships.

Clarity Through Contrast Worksheet
Janice
My Ideal Relationship

So, what do I want?

Contrast – *things I don't like* (Side A)	Clarity – *things I like* (Side B)
1. Controlling	
2. Poor listener	
3. Not affectionate	
4. Doesn't care what I think or how I feel	
5. Not outgoing	
6. Doesn't like traveling	
7. Always rushes me	
8. Makes decisions without me	
9. Doesn't like movies or dancing	

Janice made her contrast list on Side A. She recalled three past relationships during this exercise and took a couple of days to build her list.

Clarity Through Contrast Worksheet
Janice
My Ideal Relationship

So, what do I want?

Contrast – *things I don't like* (Side A)	Clarity – *things I like* (Side B)
1. ~~Controlling~~	1. Flexible, well-balanced
2. ~~Poor listener~~	2. Great listening skills
3. ~~Not affectionate~~	3. Affectionate, sensitive
4. ~~Doesn't care what I think or how I feel~~	4. Asks me what I think and how I feel about things
5. ~~Not outgoing~~	5. He likes to meet my friends and enjoys them
6. ~~Doesn't like traveling~~	6. Enjoys social situations. Loves short-term and long-term travel, likes adventure and exploring new places together
7. ~~Always rushes me~~	7. Has patience, allows things to unfold in due time
8. ~~Makes decisions without me~~	8. Asks for my ideas in decision making
9. ~~Doesn't like movies or dancing~~	9. Enjoys theater, movies, loves live bands and entertainment, likes dancing

Janice read each item on her list and asked herself "So, what do I want?" After she wrote the answer on Side B, she struck a line through the matching contrast on Side A.

Note: In our example we have listed 9 items on Janice's list. This exercise is most effective when you add as many items as possible to your contrast list (50-100 items). The more contrast you identify, the more clarity you'll generate.

Greg – Money

Greg, 27, is just barely making ends meet. He constantly complains about not having enough money. In fact, he says he's feeling stressed out about his financial situation. Greg is a self-employed consultant and business advisor, and he's having a really hard time getting and keeping clients.

He has decided to use the Law of Attraction to attract his ideal financial situation.

The Deliberate Attraction process starts with Step One, Identify Your Desire, by using the Clarity Through Contrast Worksheet. Take a look at Greg's worksheet on the next page.

Remember, in Greg's example we've listed a total of 10 items on his contrast list. This exercise is most effective when you add as many items as possible to your contrast list (50-100 items). The more contrast you identify, the more clarity you'll generate.

Clarity Through Contrast Worksheet
Greg
My Ideal Financial Situation

So, what do I want?

Contrast – *things I don't like* (Side A)	Clarity – *things I like* (Side B)
1. Not enough money	
2. Always bills to pay	
3. Just making ends meet	
4. I can't afford anything I want	
5. Money flow is sporadic	
6. I never win anything	
7. I'll always make the same amount of money	
8. Money does not come easily in my family	
9. I always struggle to pay the rent	
10. Money issues stress me	

Greg made his contrast list on Side A. He recalled his entire financial picture in the last year and took two hours to build this list. He could have taken days to complete the list if he had wanted to.

Note: In our example we have listed 10 items on Greg's list. This exercise is most effective when you add as many items as possible to your contrast list (50-100 items). The more contrast you identify, the more clarity you'll generate.

Clarity Through Contrast Worksheet
Greg
My Ideal Financial Situation

So, what do I want?

Contrast – *things I don't like* (Side A)	Clarity – *things I like* (Side B)
1. ~~Not enough money~~	1. An abundance of money
2. ~~Always bills to pay~~	2. Bills are paid easily and quickly
3. ~~Just making ends meet~~	3. Always have excess money
4. ~~I can't afford anything I want~~	4. Always have enough money to purchase whatever I desire
5. ~~Money flow is sporadic~~	5. Constant flow of money is coming in from multiple sources
6. ~~I never win anything~~	6. I win prizes often; receive gifts and many free things
7. ~~I'll always make the same amount of money~~	7. I am constantly increasing my amount of monetary intake from known and unknown sources
8. ~~Money does not come easily in my family~~	8. Money comes easily to me
9. ~~I always struggle to pay the rent~~	9. Rent is paid easily as I always have money
10. ~~Money issues stress me~~	10. Money and my relationship with it feels good

Greg read each item on his list and asked himself "So, what do I want?" After he wrote the answer on Side B, he struck a line through the matching contrast on Side A.

Complete Your Own
Clarity Through Contrast Worksheet

Choose an area in your life that you would like to change.

On Side A, list all of the things that are troubling you about your situation. For example, if you are building a contrast list about your ideal career, your list may include "the hours are too long" or "the pay is too low." Feel free to refer to a number of past jobs to help you build your list.

Take lots of time to complete this contrast list. Remember, adding more items to your contrast list will give you more clarity. I suggest you add 50-100 items. Construct it over a few days to ensure that you have thought of all the relevant episodes of contrast.

After you have completed building the contrast list on Side A, read each item and ask yourself "So, what do I want?" and complete Side B of the worksheet.

By using this Clarity Through Contrast Worksheet you will have a better understanding of what you do want (clarity of desire), by listing what you don't want (contrast). After you have reached clarity, simply cross off the matching item of contrast.

Clarity Through Contrast Worksheet
My Ideal _____

> So, what do I want?

Contrast – *things I don't like* (Side A)	Clarity – *things I like* (Side B)
List the things you don't like	List the things you would like

For more copies of this worksheet, go to
www.LawofAttractionBook.com/worksheets.html

Clarity Through Contrast Worksheet
My Ideal _____

So, what do I want?

Contrast – *things I don't like* (Side A)	Clarity – *things I like* (Side B)

Wrapping Up Step 1: Identify Your Desire

You have completed the first step of Deliberate Attraction –
Identify Your Desire.

Here's what we've covered in this section

- Your words generate a vibration that is either positive
  or negative.
- When you use the words **don't**, **not** and **no** you continue
  to give more attention, energy and focus to what you are
  referring to.
- When you hear yourself saying **don't**, **not** and **no** ask
  yourself "So, what do I want?"
- When you go from what you don't want to what you do
  want, the words change, and when the words change your
  vibration changes.
- You can only send out one vibration at a time.
- You can *reset* your vibration simply by changing your words,
  remembering that thoughts are made up of words.
- Contrast is anything that doesn't feel good.
- Observe contrast briefly knowing that the Law of Attraction
  is always responding to your vibration.
- Use contrast to help generate clarity.
- When building your contrast list find as many contrast
  items as possible. The more contrast you identify, the more
  clarity you'll have.

Remember, you've only pinpointed your desire at this point.
You may have felt great about identifying and writing down
what you want or you may have experienced a feeling of doubt.

In the following chapters, you'll learn how to continue on with
the Law of Attraction formula using Step 2 and Step 3.

Step 2 - Give Your Desire Attention

Giving Attention Increases Vibration

To raise (increase) your vibration simply means to give your desire more positive attention, energy and focus.

It is not enough to merely identify your desire; you must also give it positive attention. Giving it positive attention ensures that you are including the vibration of your desire in your current vibration.

The Law of Attraction brings you more of whatever you give your attention, energy and focus to. If, however, you identify your desire and don't give it attention, energy and focus, then there is no manifestation. The key here is to identify your desire and continue to give it attention. As you're giving it attention, you are now including the vibration of your desire in your current vibration. Your current vibration is what the Law of Attraction responds to.

Some people are good at identifying their desires and then they tuck their list of desires away and never give it attention again. The Law of Attraction can only respond to what you're giving your attention to.

The next section of this book explains this concept using the idea that we have a Vibrational Bubble around us, where all of our current vibration is stored. You must be sure to include the vibration of your desire in your current Vibrational Bubble.

What am I Including in My Vibrational Bubble?

Imagine that you have a bubble that is surrounding you and captured within this bubble are all the vibrations you are sending out. The Law of Attraction is responding to whatever is *inside* your Vibrational Bubble.

Are your desires inside or outside your Vibrational Bubble?

It is important to understand that all your goals, dreams and desires are outside of your Vibrational Bubble. If they were inside your Vibrational Bubble you would already have them and be enjoying them. Take, for example, the exercise you completed in Step 1 to identify your new desire. Now that you have new clarity about your desire, it's necessary to include that vibration in your current vibration because that's what the Law of Attraction responds to. If you build your desire list and put it away in your sock drawer, your desire won't manifest because the Law of Attraction doesn't respond to things in a sock drawer. It only responds to what is currently in your Vibrational Bubble.

In Step 2 of the Deliberate Attraction process you will learn how to use words to give attention, energy and focus to your new desires by creating a Desire Statement. While you are sustaining that attention, energy and focus on your desire, you are including it in your current Vibrational Bubble where the Law of Attraction responds to and matches that vibration.

What do You include in Your Vibrational Bubble?

Am I Including It or Excluding It From My Vibrational Bubble?

Using the worksheet on the following page, determine which column each of the following sentences will go in.

- When I'm talking about what I desire
- When I'm noticing something I like
- When I'm daydreaming about my desire
- When I visualize my desire
- When I'm pretending I already have my desire
- When I say yes to something
- When I say no to something
- When I worry about something
- When I complain about something
- When I remember something positive
- When I remember something negative
- When I'm observing something positive
- When I'm observing something negative
- When I'm playing with the idea of having my desire
- When I'm making a collage about my desire
- When I'm praying about my desire
- When I'm celebrating something I like

*What am I
including in my
Vibrational Bubble?*

My Vibrational Bubble – Worksheet

Action that INCLUDES it in my Vibrational Bubble.	Action that EXCLUDES it from my Vibrational Bubble.

You'll find a completed worksheet on the following page.

My Vibrational Bubble – Worksheet

Action that INCLUDES it in my Vibrational Bubble.	Action that EXCLUDES it from my Vibrational Bubble.
• talking about my desire • noticing something I like • daydreaming about my desire • visualizing my desire • pretending I have my desire • when I say yes to something • when I say no to something • when I worry about something • when I complain about something • when I remember something positive • when I remember something negative • when I'm observing something positive • when I'm observing something negative • when I'm playing with the idea of having my desire • when I'm making a collage about my desire • when I'm praying about my desire • when I'm celebrating something I like	Can you see how everything gets included?

Notice that when you say "No" to something, you just gave it attention, energy and focus. In that moment, it also becomes included in your Vibrational Bubble. Giving anything *attention of any kind* includes it in your current vibration.

Two Tools for Raising Your Vibration to Fuel Your Desire

One of the keys to make the Law of Attraction work for you lies in keeping your desires within your current vibration, i.e., your Vibrational Bubble.

In the next few pages I'll explain how affirmations may or may not be helping you include your desire in your Vibrational Bubble and I'll give you a great tool that can help you reword your affirmations so they DO work. Also, I'll introduce you to another tool I call the "Desire Statement." This effective tool ensures that you are including and keeping your new desire in your Vibrational Bubble. It is especially useful when dealing with new desires that may be forgotten if not given deliberate attention.

First let me explain why using affirmations may not be raising your vibration.

Why Using Affirmations May Not Raise Your Vibration

An affirmation is a statement spoken in the present tense and used to declare a desire. Saying "I have a happy, slender body," is an example of a positive affirmation.

Each time you read your affirmation you'll have a reaction based upon how the words make you feel. Remember, the Law of Attraction responds to the vibrations you send out based on how you feel, not based on specific words you use. If, for example, you tell yourself that you have a happy, slender body when you do not, or when having a happy, slender body feels unattainable, you'll create negative vibrations. You'll send out a vibration of doubt (a negative vibration), which the Law of Attraction will respond to by giving you more of the same, even though it's unwanted.

A positive affirmation can have a negative vibration. Most affirmations don't work because the Law of Attraction doesn't respond to words – it responds to how you feel about the words you use.

On the following page you'll see a list of positive affirmations.

After reading each statement, ask yourself which vibration you are sending, negative or positive.

+	—	Vibration
☐	☐	All my family relationships are harmonious
☐	☐	I love my body
☐	☐	I'm a millionaire
☐	☐	My business is booming
☐	☐	I have ideal health
☐	☐	I have a perfect life mate

Question: When would these affirmations offer a positive vibration?

Answer: When they are true for you!

When you state something that is *not* true for you, you are offering a negative vibration because the statement activates doubt within you. As you state the affirmation, a part of you says:

◆ That's not true, my family relationships aren't harmonious
◆ That's not true, I don't love my body
◆ That's not true, I'm not a millionaire yet
◆ That's not true, my business isn't booming
◆ That's not true, I don't have ideal health
◆ That's not true, I don't have a perfect life mate

The key to using affirmations is that they need to be true for you in order to make you feel good. On the following page I'll give you a tool to help you reword an affirmation so it is ALWAYS true for you, thus enabling you to send out a positive vibration.

The Law of Attraction responds to how you feel about what you say and how you feel about what you think.

Tool #1: Rewording Your Affirmations to Make Them Feel Better

Some of you have been taught to always state your affirmations in the current tense. Here, I'm suggesting that you are *in the process*. "The process" (the process of manifestation), actually starts when you think about your desire, talk about it, write about it, or when you give it ANY kind of attention, energy and focus. So the truth is you ARE in the process. When you say "I'm in the process of…," that sentence becomes true and if it's true for you, it feels good, which is a positive vibration.

Let's revisit the statements on the previous page, starting each sentence with the following:

I'm in the process of…

◆ I'm in the process of creating ideal family relationships
◆ I'm in the process of enjoying my body more and more
◆ I'm in the process of becoming more abundant
◆ I'm in the process of growing my business
◆ I'm in the process of having ideal health
◆ I'm in the process of attracting an ideal mate

Now each statement is true for you! When a statement is true for you it feels good. When it feels good, you are sending a positive vibration which the Law of Attraction responds to by bringing you more of the same.

Tool #2: The Desire Statement Tool

A Desire Statement is an effective tool for raising your vibration and is the second step in the 3-step process of Deliberate Attraction. Once you're clear about what you want, writing a Desire Statement helps you give attention to that desire. Remember, the Law of Attraction states whatever you give your attention, energy and focus to you'll get more of, and the Desire Statement lets you do just that.

For example, you might say "I want to own my own home." In that moment, the Law of Attraction is orchestrating circumstances and events to bring it to you. However, if you're like most people, you'll probably sabotage yourself by saying you can't afford your own home. Now you're offering a vibration of lack and that's what the Law of Attraction is responding to.

Once you've written your Desire Statement, you will experience feelings of excitement, possibility and hope, all of which are a sign that your vibration has been raised – you can tell by how you feel.

There are three elements to the Desire Statement:

◆ The opening sentence
◆ The body (your Clarity list from Step 1)
◆ The closing sentence

In the following section you'll learn how to use these three elements to create your Desire Statement.

Desire Statement - Opening sentence

I am in the process of attracting all that I need to do, know, or have, to attract my ideal desire.

Desire Statement - Body

Using the statements from your Clarity list, combine them with these phrases:

I love knowing that my ideal _____

I love how it feels when _____

I've decided _____

More and more _____

It excites me _____

I love the idea of _____

I'm excited at the thought of _____

I love seeing myself _____

Examples:

- ◆ I love knowing that my ideal partner lives in my city.
- ◆ I love how it feels when I'm doing a bank deposit for my business.
- ◆ I'm excited at the thought of traveling with my ideal mate.
- ◆ I love the idea of having a full client base.
- ◆ I love seeing myself making healthy food choices.

The above phrases allow you to talk about your desire and at the same time knowing it is true for you. You DO love knowing, or love the thought of, or love seeing yourself, etc.. Now you are including a positive vibration about your desire and including it in your Vibrational Bubble. Using the word *ideal* is important here. Referring to an ideal mate, or ideal health, or ideal career, allows you to talk about it *now*, thus enabling you to include it in your current vibration. Remember, the purpose of the Desire Statement is to help you include your new desire in your Vibrational Bubble.

Can you feel the difference in vibration between:

> I love knowing that my *ideal* relationship is nurturing and uplifting.

> AND

> My relationships are nurturing and uplifting.

In the first statement you're saying that your *ideal* relationship is nurturing and uplifting and this applies whether you're in one or not. Your vibration is positive. Again, you aren't stating that you have your *ideal* relationship right now, but you are saying that you are clear about desiring these attributes that make up your *ideal* relationship.

The second statement is an assertion that you already have nurturing and uplifting relationships. If that isn't true for you, you'll have doubt, which generates a negative vibration.

Desire Statement - Closing sentence

The Law of Attraction is unfolding and orchestrating all that needs to happen to bring me my desire.

Examples of Completed Desire Statements

Before you write your own Desire Statement, let's look at the examples for Janice and Greg. Remember, Janice and Greg's first step was to build a list of contrast (dislikes), to help them become clear about their desires. I've included their Clarity Through Contrast Worksheets here to help show how it helped them create their Desire Statement.

Clarity Through Contrast Worksheet
Janice
My Ideal Relationship

So, what do I want?

Contrast – *things I don't like* (Side A)	Clarity – *things I like* (Side B)
1. ~~Controlling~~	1. Flexible, well-balanced
2. ~~Poor listener~~	2. Great listening skills
3. ~~Not affectionate~~	3. Affectionate, sensitive
4. ~~Doesn't care what I think or how I feel~~	4. Asks me what I think and how I feel about things
5. ~~Not outgoing~~	5. He likes to meet my friends and enjoys them
6. ~~Doesn't like traveling~~	6. Enjoys social situations. Loves short-term and long-term travel, likes adventure and exploring new places together
7. ~~Always rushes me~~	7. Has patience; allows things to unfold in due time
8. ~~Makes decisions without me~~	8. Asks for my ideas in decision making
9. ~~Doesn't like movies or dancing~~	9. Enjoys theater, movies, loves live bands and entertainment; likes dancing

To build her Desire Statement, Janice took her Clarity list and plugged it into the Desire Statement model.

Janice's Desire Statement
My Ideal Relationship

Opening sentence

I am in the process of attracting all that I need to do, know or have to attract my ideal relationship.

Body

I love how it feels knowing that my ideal relationship is with a man who is flexible and well-balanced. He has great listening skills and enjoys conversations.

I love how it feels knowing that my ideal partner is affectionate and sensitive and asks about my feelings. I love being asked to be included in decision-making opportunities.

I love knowing that my ideal partner enjoys and looks forward to meeting my friends in social situations. My partner and I enjoy short-term and long-term travel together, experiencing trips and vacations that bring us closer.

I've decided that my ideal partner is patient, caring, gentle and allows things to unfold in due time. It feels great to be asked by my ideal partner what I think and feel about things and to have balanced conversations where each of us is included. I love asking my partner for input and I love being asked.

I'm excited at the thought of enjoying the theatre, movies, live entertainment and dancing with my ideal partner. I love being adored by my ideal partner and I love that my ideal partner enjoys being adored. He is optimistic and loves being uplifted. He's supportive and supportable.

Closing sentence

The Law of Attraction is unfolding and orchestrating all that needs to happen to bring me my desire.

Clarity Through Contrast Worksheet
Greg
My Ideal Financial Situation

So, what do I want?

Contrast – *things I don't like* (Side A)	Clarity – *things I like* (Side B)
1. ~~Not enough money~~	1. Abundance of money
2. ~~Always bills to pay~~	2. Bills are paid easily and quickly
3. ~~Just making ends meet~~	3. Always have excess money
4. ~~I can't afford anything I want~~	4. Always have enough money to purchase whatever I desire
5. ~~Money flow is sporadic~~	5. Constant flow of money is coming in from multiple sources
6. ~~I never win anything~~	6. I win prizes often; receive gifts and many free things
7. ~~I'll always make the same amount of money~~	7. I am constantly increasing my amount of monetary intake from known and unknown sources
8. ~~Money does not come easily in my family~~	8. Money comes easily to me
9. ~~I always struggle to pay the rent~~	9. Rent is paid easily as I always have money
10. ~~Money issues stress me~~	10. Money and my relationship with it feels good

Greg's Desire Statement
My Ideal Financial Situation

Opening sentence

I am in the process of attracting all that I need to do, know or have to attract my ideal financial situation.

Body

I love knowing that my ideal financial situation allows me to have and enjoy everything that I need and desire to bring more joy and freedom to my life.

Abundance is a feeling and I love the feeling of abundance all around me. I love knowing that all my bills are paid with joy, knowing that what I am billed for is an exchange, using money to honor that exchange.

I'm so excited at the thought of a constant flow of money coming to me from known and unknown sources.

I love knowing that my ideal financial situation brings me the comfort and the knowledge that I can travel where I want, shop where I want, and have whatever will make me feel great.

More and more, I receive gifts, win more prizes, and receive what I need from unknown and known sources.

I love the thought of stashing money away into excellent investments.

Closing sentence

The Law of Attraction is unfolding and orchestrating all that needs to happen to bring me my desire.

How to Create Your Desire Statement

Now it's your turn to create your own Desire Statement.

Use the items on your completed Clarity Through Contrast Worksheet to build the body of your Desire Statement on the following worksheet.

I have provided you with the opening and closing sentences. All you have to do is fill in the body.

Use some or all of the following phrases to help describe your ideal desire:

I love knowing that my ideal _____

I love how it feels when _____

I've decided _____

More and more _____

It excites me _____

I love the idea of _____

I'm excited at the thought of _____

I love seeing myself _____

There are two blank worksheets on the following pages. For more copies, go to www.LawofAttractionBook.com/worksheets.html

Desire Statement Worksheet

Desire Statement
My Ideal _____

I am in the process of attracting all that I need to do, know or have to attract my ideal

_____

_____

_____

_____

_____

_____

_____

_____

_____

_____

_____

The Law of Attraction is unfolding and orchestrating all that needs to happen to bring me my desire.

Desire Statement Worksheet

Desire Statement
My Ideal _____

I am in the process of attracting all that I need to do, know or have to attract my ideal

_____

_____

_____

_____

_____

_____

_____

_____

_____

_____

_____

The Law of Attraction is unfolding and orchestrating all that needs to happen to bring me my desire.

How Do I Know If I'm Doing It Right?

After you've written your Desire Statement, go back and read
it. Next, ask yourself how you feel. Do you hear a little negative
voice or have an uncomfortable feeling? Does your Desire
Statement make you feel great? If not, then revise your statement
so that you feel better (raise your vibration) when you read it.
Remember, the purpose of the Desire Statement is to raise your
vibration to help you include your new desire in your Vibrational
Bubble.

Wrapping up Step 2:
Give Your Desire Attention

You have completed the second phase of Deliberate Attraction –
Giving your desire attention.

Here's what we've covered in this section

◆ Your Vibrational Bubble contains all of your current
  vibrations.
◆ You must include the vibration of your new desire in your
  current Vibrational Bubble.
◆ A Desire Statement helps you include the vibration of your
  desire in your Vibrational Bubble.
◆ The purpose of Step 2 is to give your desire attention.
◆ You raise your vibration when you give your desire
  attention, energy and focus.
◆ Your affirmations may not feel good when the statements
  aren't true for you.
◆ Law of Attraction responds to how you feel about your
  affirmations.

Now that you've completed Step 1 and Step 2 of the Law of
Attraction formula, it's time to apply the third step – Allowing.

3 STEPS Identify Your Desire
Give Your Desire Attention
Allow It

Step 3 - Allow It

It's All About Allowing

Now some of you may be saying "I've had desires in the past that I got excited about and they never resulted in anything." Remember, Deliberate Attraction is a 3-step process.

You've identified your desire and given it your attention. The third step in the Deliberate Attraction process is 'Allowing'. Let's get started.

Allowing is simply the absence of negative vibration and doubt is a negative vibration. Allowing is the most important step in the Deliberate Attraction process. One of my clients, Danny, asked me why he did not attract his desires. He had built a great Clarity list of his ideal clients and made an awesome Desire Statement that felt great. So why didn't he attract his desires?

The process didn't work for him because it was not enough for him to just identify his desire and really want it. He also had to remove any doubt surrounding his belief that he would attract it. This doubt-removing process is called Allowing.

You may have heard the expression "Just allow it." Telling yourself this doesn't help you to allow. If you doubt you can have something, you are sending a negative vibration. This negative vibration is diluting or cancelling the positive vibration of your desire. In other words, having strong desire (positive vibe), and having strong doubt (negative vibe), cancel each other out. Therefore, Allowing occurs in the absence of doubt.

Allowing is the absence of negative vibration (doubt).

You know you are Allowing something when you hear yourself saying statements such as:

◆ "Ah, what a relief!"
◆ "You know, maybe I can have this."
◆ "Now this feels possible."

In all three of the above expressions, what you are actually describing is the feeling of the negative vibration being removed.

Most people say that Allowing is the most difficult step in the Law of Attraction formula. It's not the most difficult step; it's just the least understood. Most people don't understand how to allow so they become frustrated when people say "Just allow it."

In this section, I'll give you *how-to tools* to help you allow.

The Allowing Game

Here is a model to help you understand the importance of Allowing, as illustrated by a simple children's game.

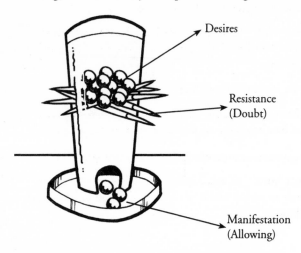

Desires

Resistance
(Doubt)

Manifestation
(Allowing)

Here's how the game works. A number of marbles rest on sticks that criss-cross through a clear cylinder. The sticks represent resistance/doubt, the marbles represent desire, and the fallen marbles represent manifestation (Allowing).

In the course of the game, the sticks are removed allowing some marbles to fall to the bottom of the cylinder.

As you can see in the diagram, the only way the marbles will fall is if the sticks are removed. In the same way, having a strong desire is not enough – it is only when your resistance is removed that your desire is manifested. The faster your resistance/doubt is removed, the faster your desire can be realized.

In other words, the speed at which the Law of Attraction manifests your desire is in direct proportion to how much you are Allowing.

Here are a couple of questions to ponder:

Does having strong desire make your desire manifest faster?
Do you have to remove all your doubt to manifest your desire?

The following illustrations will answer these questions.

In other words, the speed at which the Law of Attraction responds to your desire is in direct proportion to how much you allow.

The Power of Allowing

Having a strong desire with strong doubt means your desire will not be manifested.

Having a strong desire with just a little bit of doubt means your desire will come, though slowly.

Having a strong desire with no doubt means your desire will be manifested quickly.

Although smiling, these lottery ticket purchasers have thoughts of doubt about winning.

If you have a strong desire and strong doubt, your desire will come slowly to you, if at all. The speed at which you'll win the lottery (your desire) is determined by how much doubt you have. Do you have doubts?

The speed at which Law of Attraction manifests your desire is in direct proportion to how much you Allow.

Where Does Doubt Come From?

The most common source of doubt (negative vibration) is from your own limiting beliefs.

What is a Limiting Belief?

A limiting belief is a repetitive thought that you think over and over, and over again. When your thoughts consist of a limiting belief you are offering or sending out a negative vibration. That negative vibration is preventing you from attracting your desire. The phrase "I have to work hard to make money" vibrates lack, which stops you from getting what you want.

How Can You Identify Your Limiting Beliefs?

Here's an easy way to identify your limiting beliefs. They are usually found after you say the word *because*, as in the phrase, "*I can't because…*"

Here are some examples:

- I'd like to write a book but I can't *because* I don't have a university degree.
- I'd like to start my own business but I can't *because* I'm too old.
- I'd like to have a more slender body but it's so hard *because* everybody in my family is overweight.
- I'd like to have an ideal mate but I can't *because* I'm too fat, too old or too shy, etc.

Let's go back to our two case studies with Janice and Greg. Janice's desire was to attract her ideal relationship. She caught herself saying that she couldn't attract an ideal partner *because* she was too old. And Greg caught himself saying that he couldn't be financially wealthy *because* he comes from a poor family.

So what are your limiting beliefs? When you catch yourself saying the word *because*, you've just discovered one of your limiting beliefs.

In this section, you'll learn how to use tools that will assist you in changing your limiting beliefs.

Allowing is the absence of negative vibration. Doubt is a negative vibration and doubt is often created from limiting beliefs.

A Tool to Help You Allow

There are a number of tools for Allowing. The first one we're going to explore is Allowing Statements. The purpose of Allowing Statements is to lessen or remove any doubt that is preventing you from receiving what you want. After making your Allowing Statements you will experience a feeling of relief. That is, you will believe that you really are going to attract what you desire. Believing is also the absence of doubt, as is faith.

Two Ways to Know You've Allowed

Remembering that Allowing is the absence of negative vibration, there are two ways you can tell if you are allowing:

◆ First, you can tell by how you feel. When you remove a negative feeling of resistance, most people feel a sense of relief or hear themselves saying "Ah, this feels much better!"

◆ The second way that you can tell is by noticing when manifestation appears in your life. When evidence is showing up in your life, you know you are allowing.

In the following pages you'll learn how to change your thoughts to positive ones. Offering these new positive thoughts over and over again will then create your new beliefs. Remember, a limiting belief is simply a repetitive thought you think over and over again, therefore, any belief can be changed.

Formula for Creating Allowing Statements

Whenever you hear yourself stating a limiting belief (or having doubt), you can use this formula to help create an Allowing Statement which will help lessen or remove your doubt.

Writing your own Allowing Statements is simple.

◆ Start by asking yourself if there is anyone currently doing what you want to do or having what you want?
◆ If so, then how many people have been doing this today? Yesterday? Last week? Last month? Last year?
◆ Write your statements in general terms (3rd person), because making reference to yourself may create more doubt.
◆ Ensure that the statements are plausible.

Here is an example of how to create Allowing Statements for the following limiting beliefs.

Limiting Belief #1:

I'd like to have a more slender body but I can't because all my family members are big.

Question: Is there anyone on the planet who has a different body size than other members of their family?

Answer: Yes

Question: If so, how many people have this today? Yesterday? Last week? Last month? Last year?

Allowing Statement:

Thousands of people, even in my neighbourhood, have different body sizes than their family members. There are millions of men on the planet that have a more slender body than their father or brother. (Note: This sentence is written in general terms, in the 3rd person, to exclude making any reference to yourself.)

Limiting Belief #2:

I'd like to start my own business but I can't because I'm 50 years old!

Question: Is there anyone my age on the planet that has started their own business?

Answer: Yes

Question: If so, then how many people have been doing this today? Yesterday? Last week? Last month? Last year?

Allowing Statement:

Right now there are hundreds of people in their fifties who are starting and running successful businesses. There are millions of 50-year-old (plus) successful business owners.

Write your Allowing Statements in general terms (3rd person), because making reference to yourself may create more doubt.

Now, let's return to Janice and Greg to see how they created their Allowing Statements.

As you'll recall, Janice is tired and frustrated because she continually has the wrong kind of man showing interest in her. She complains that she attracts men who are unavailable, insensitive and who never make her a priority.

Janice is using Deliberate Attraction to help her attract her ideal relationship. She is clear about her desires and is already using a Desire Statement. Because this is a new desire for her, she has to lessen the doubt in order to receive it. She does this by composing Allowing Statements.

Janice's Allowing Statements
My Ideal Relationship

◆ Hundreds of people met their ideal partner last month.
◆ Thousands of people are on first dates today with a person who will become their lifelong ideal partner.
◆ Hundreds of thousands of couples are enjoying each other's company today.
◆ Millions of couples are in their ideal relationship.
◆ Every day more and more people are attracting their ideal partners.
◆ Millions of couples are doing social activities together that include travelling and vacations.
◆ Hundreds of thousands of couples will go dancing this week.

As Janice reads her Allowing Statements, she begins to feel hope and the reduction of doubt. Now, the Law of Attraction can bring Janice her ideal mate.

Remember Greg? He's the self-employed consultant and business advisor who's having a really hard time making ends meet. He constantly complains about not having enough money. In fact, he says he's feeling pretty stressed out about his financial situation.

Greg is using Deliberate Attraction to help him attract his ideal financial situation. He is clear about his desires and is already using a Desire Statement. Because this is a new desire for him, he has to lessen and remove the doubt in order to manifest. He does this by composing Allowing Statements.

Greg's Allowing Statements
My Ideal Financial Situation

◆ Millions of people are receiving checks today.
◆ Every day, billions of dollars are moved from bank account to bank account.
◆ Someone just received a check this minute.
◆ Hundreds of thousands of people win prizes and money every day.
◆ Somebody became a millionaire yesterday.
◆ Millions of dollars are inherited every day.
◆ Someone found money today.
◆ More and more people are attracting creative ways to bring in extra income.

As Greg reads his Allowing Statements he begins to feel hope and the diminishing of doubt. Now the Law of Attraction can respond to Greg's desire for his ideal financial situation.

How to Create Your Own Allowing Statement

It's time for you to create your own Allowing Statement. The Allowing Statement is used when you hear yourself make statements of doubt. Build a list of these doubts. You may hear yourself saying "I can't have that *because*…," or "That won't happen to me *because*…!" You can use the Allowing Statements worksheet on the next page to help build your Allowing Statements.

1st STEP: Uncover the Doubt

Reread your Desire Statement and use it to uncover any doubt you feel as a result of reading it. For example, if your desire statement says that your ideal job allows you to work a 4-day week and you hear a little voice inside you saying "That will never happen because…," then jot down your doubt.

2nd STEP: Ask Yourself These Questions

Start by asking yourself whether there is anyone currently doing what you want to do or having what you want to have. If so, then how many people have been doing this today? Yesterday? Last week? Last month? Last year?

3rd STEP: Write in General Terms (in the 3rd person)

Write your statements in general terms because making reference to yourself often creates more doubt. Ensure that the statements are plausible.

Allowing Statements
My Ideal _____

_____

_____

_____

_____

_____

_____

_____

_____

_____

_____

_____

For more copies of this worksheet, go to
www.LawofAttractionBook.com/worksheets.html

There are two ways to tell when you are Allowing.

First, you feel a sense of relief and often hear yourself saying "Ah! This feels much better."

Second, you see evidence of your manifestation appearing in your life.

More Tools to Help You Allow

In addition to the Allowing Statement Tool, here are additional tools.

1. Celebrate the Proof (Evidence)
2. Record Your Proof of the Law of Attraction
3. Appreciation and Gratitude
4. Use the Expression, "I'm in the Process of…"
5. Use the Expression, "I've Decided…"
6. Use the Expression, "Lots Can Happen…"
7. Ask for Information
8. Make Yourself an Attraction Box
9. Create a Void or Vacuum
10. Allow the Law of Attraction to figure it out

*Remember, it's the
absence of doubt
that will bring
your desire faster.*

Tool #1: Celebrate the Proof (Evidence)

Remember that to manifest your desire you need to remove the doubt. Doubt is what stops your desire from coming to you. The best way to remove doubt is to find proof. Scientists, for example, only believe something after it's been proven. Like most of us, when someone proves something to us, we often say "Okay, I believe it now. I can see the proof." Here's how to use proof (evidence) to your advantage.

Have you noticed when something you desire starts showing up in your life, even just a little bit, it excites you? For example, you attract a bit of information you've been looking for, or you meet someone who is a pretty close match to your ideal partner or your ideal client. All of this is proof (evidence) of the Law of Attraction at work in your life.

How you observe proof (evidence) of the Law of Attraction is important. In some cases, people might say "Oh, this isn't exactly what I want," or "He's not quite the right person I was looking for," or "It's kind of close but not really." Saying or thinking these kinds of phrases creates a negative vibration.

When you find and experience proof (evidence) of the Law of Attraction, celebrate it by acknowledging how close you came to getting what you desired. It's in the celebration of the closeness of the match that you offer more vibration of what you desire, and at that moment, the Law of Attraction is responding to your vibration. Remember, the Law of Attraction does not care whether you are remembering, pretending, playing, creating, complaining or worrying. It simply responds to your vibration and sends you more of the same. So find proof and rejoice.

Janice, who is using the Law of Attraction to attract her ideal relationship, is a great example of how this tool can be used to lessen doubt.

Shortly after Janice completed her Desire Statement and started using the Allowing tools, she met a man who was a visitor to her city. They hit it off right away. They had lots in common including a love of music, theatre, and movies. She was really impressed by his good communication skills and how upbeat he was. Three days later, Janice called me and I could hear some disappointment in her voice. She spent lots of time and attention describing her disappointment that he was from another country (thus, including what she didn't want in her Vibrational Bubble). Yet I knew he was a close match to her desire and that she was not acknowledging that fact. My job was to help her include all those things that were a match in her Vibrational Bubble.

Here's how I used this tool with Janice. I simply asked her to tell me all the things about her new relationship that excited her. In other words, the things that were in her Desire Statement that made her feel great. She quickly built a list that included his great communication skills; his love of music, theatre, and movies; his values; and how happy she felt around him. Janice could feel her vibration rise the moment she started creating this list. Finding and celebrating the closeness of the match shifted her vibration immediately. As Janice began recalling and noticing the closeness of the match she was once again including this vibration in her Vibrational Bubble.

And you know how the Law of Attraction responds to that!

Tool #2: Record Proof of the Law of Attraction

Keeping a diary or a Book of Proof of the Law of Attraction in your life will help you believe it more, get excited more, allow more, and trust more. Regardless of the size of the manifestation (e.g., you found a quarter or you won a prize), if it's something you desired – log it! Record your proof and you will raise your vibration.

Finding proof helps lessens doubt. Remember that any time you've ever had something proven to you, in that very moment, all doubt is removed. You might have heard yourself saying "NOW I believe that!"

After a couple of pages of recording proof you will realize how much the Law of Attraction is really working in your life. As you use the Law of Attraction more knowingly, you will have confirmation that will help you trust the process of Allowing more easily, thus lessening the doubt (resistance). Remember, it's the absence of doubt that will bring your desire faster.

So whenever you're feeling doubtful about the Law of Attraction, you just need to read your Book of Proof. Reading your Book of Proof will remind you of the evidence you've received and will lower or remove your doubt.

Example of a Book of Proof

Date: _____

Today I observed this proof (evidence)

Money left in parking meter	Free parking validation ticket
I was treated to lunch today	Free sample at coffee shop
Got 30% off a purchase	Was given free advice over dinner

Book of Proof

Date: _____
Today I observed this proof (evidence)

Date: _____
Today I observed this proof (evidence)

Date: _____
Today I observed this proof (evidence)

For more copies of this worksheet, go to
www.LawofAttractionBook.com/worksheets.html

The Book of Proof Worked for Ivor

Being analytically minded (I work in the financial business), I figured I was the most unlikely person to get involved with the Law of Attraction. But through Michael's teachings, I learned how to change my thoughts and be open and receptive to new ideas. Then wonderful things began to happen. I started taking an optimistic approach to business situations that I would generally worry about. When I deliberately raised my vibration from worry to a positive, happy mood, I noticed that I got results – and they came fast. If I decided I wanted to meet three new clients in one day, that's what happened! One of the ways I log proof of how the Law of Attraction is working for me is I use my Book of Proof to record all my successes, both big and small. I record when I am successful in getting a referral, a new client, paying off a bill or receiving a big check, etc. I refer to my book often – whenever I want to raise my vibration and remind myself how powerful the Law of Attraction is.

Ivor John
Financial Advisor
Victoria, BC

Remember, the Law of Attraction does not care whether you are remembering, pretending, celebrating, playing, creating, complaining or worrying.

It simply responds to what's in your Vibrational Bubble.

So, find proof, rejoice and send out a positive vibration.

Tool #3: Appreciation and Gratitude

Appreciation and gratitude help you send out strong positive vibrations. When you're appreciating something, you're offering a feeling and vibration of pure joy. Think of a time when you expressed thanks for someone in your life. The feelings you experienced were positive.

Keeping an appreciation and gratitude journal is an effective daily tool for maintaining a positive vibration. When you purposely take time to appreciate every day you are intentionally offering strong, positive vibrations, and including those vibrations in your Vibrational Bubble.

You can take time to appreciate anything. It's the feeling that's attached to your appreciation that is important.

Janice, whose desire is an ideal relationship, keeps a daily appreciation journal. It allows her to reflect on the relationships that she loves in her life. Here are a few samples of Janice's appreciation statements:

◆ I am grateful that I went hiking with new friends this week.
◆ I loved sharing lunch today with close friends.
◆ I appreciate my close friends giving me their attention.
◆ I love having lots of friends.

While Janice is thinking and writing her daily appreciation statements, she is offering a positive vibration. In that same moment the Law of Attraction is unfolding to bring her more of what she is offering 'vibrationally.'

Take time to appreciate anything. It's the feeling that's attached to your appreciation that is important. Appreciation and gratitude help you offer strong, positive vibrations.

Tool #4: Use the Expression, "I'm in the Process of..."

Sometimes it's hard to believe you will get what you desire. This is especially true if you're focusing on the fact that you haven't reached your goal. When you concentrate on what you don't have, you're offering a negative vibration. So instead, feel the relief by saying "I'm in the process of..."

Saying you don't have something is another way of focusing on your lack and generates a negative vibration. When you catch yourself saying you don't have something yet, stop, and instead say "I'm in the process of attracting..."

Some people may ask "Then are you not always in the process of?" The answer is yes, you are always *in the process of*. The Law of Attraction is always unfolding and orchestrating events and circumstances to respond to your vibration and bring you more of the same. As you attract whatever it is you've desired, once it manifests, you'll generate a new desire and once again be *in the process of*.

In the very moment you think about a new desire, talk about it, write about it, put it on your calendar, or on a reminder note on your fridge, you have just begun *the process of* because in each of these cases, you are giving your new desire attention, energy and focus. So it is true...you are *in the process of*!

Here are some examples of how to apply the tool "I'm in the process of..."

Before: I still haven't attracted my ideal mate.
- I'm in the process of attracting my ideal mate.

Before: I'm still waiting for my ideal job.
- I'm in the process of obtaining my ideal job.

Before: I haven't reached my goal weight yet.
- I'm in the process of having a happier, slender body.

Remember to use this expression whenever you're focusing on the doubt of not reaching your goals or manifesting your desires.

Tool #5: Use the Expression, "I've Decided..."

Another way to rephrase your expressions so they offer a positive vibration is to use the phrase "I've decided." Have you noticed that in most cases when you say "I've decided..." it creates a strong positive emotion. "I've decided I'm having this," or "I've decided I'm doing that." Most people rarely use the word *decide*, yet it is an excellent way to take your focus off of lack and put it back onto your desire.

- ◆ I've decided I'm going to have more money in my life.
- ◆ I've decided I'm going to work three days a week.
- ◆ I've decided I'm going to be in a happy, healthy relationship.
- ◆ I've decided to start my own business.
- ◆ I've decided to attract my ideal job.

You may have noticed that when some people experience contrast they may declare loudly "That's enough! I've decided from now on I'm having it this way!" So deciding is really about making a decision and with that decision you send out the vibration of what you want to attract.

Decide more often. You'll feel instant relief from the positive emotions that come with each act of deciding.

Tool #6: Use the Expression, "Lots Can Happen..."

I had a client, Jason, who was using the Law of Attraction to attract his ideal customer. I could hear in his words that he was trying to determine where his next major purchaser was coming from. He was saying things like "It seems like I've been waiting forever. I wonder when this is going to happen?" Even though Jason had completed the entire 3-step process, there was still a part of him that doubted. The statements Jason was making about his next client had a negative vibration of lack (doubt).

Jason was spending a lot of energy trying to figure out why he wasn't getting what he wanted and was noticing that he wasn't reaching his goals. Like Jason, you've probably spent some time noticing you haven't reached your goals.

Here are some questions that I asked Jason to help him go from his place of not reaching his goals to a place of possibility.

- ◆ Can lots happen in the next few days?
- ◆ Can lots happen in the next week?
- ◆ Can lots happen in the next 30 days?

Jason excitedly answered "Yes" to all of these questions. The moment I reminded Jason about the phrase "Lots can happen," I could see his relief. This experience also reminded him of times when lots happened even when he doubted lots could happen. Using this Allowing phrase helped Jason shift his vibration from lack to abundance, or from a negative vibration to a positive one.

From now on, the moment you notice a lack of results, focus on the possibility that "lots can happen."

Tool #7: Ask for Information

Often when we define our desires and get excited about attracting them, the doubt we may have stops the Law of Attraction from bringing them to us. If your desire is to have a full client base, for example, you may doubt that it is possible. However, you could desire to attract information that will help you with that goal. Try it. If you feel more hopeful after you've asked for information, then you just reduced your doubts, which allows the Law of Attraction to bring your desires to you more quickly.

Example: I'd like to attract some more information on where to get started with my new desire.

- ◆ I'd like to start attracting information about my desire to get me started.
- ◆ I'd like the LAW OF ATTRACTION to bring to me some creative information on how I can manifest my desire.
- ◆ I'd like to attract some information and ideas about more ways to generate business.
- ◆ I'd like some information about where to network my new business.

We have less resistance to accepting information and as a result information comes quickly because there is no negative vibration to stop it from coming.

One of the best techniques for breaking things down is the one I used with Greg's financial situation. Even after completing the 3-step process, he still felt doubtful that he could have what he desired.

I asked Greg just to take the first step. That is, to ask for and accept any information that fit with his desire to receive more money. Greg instantly got excited and said "Oh, what a great start! I can attract information about what I need to do to attract more money. That's what I need. Now THAT I can do!"

Tool #8: Make Yourself an Attraction Box

An Attraction Box is used to collect things that represent your desire: things you've cut out of magazines and newspapers, brochures for trips you want to take, or even business cards of people you want to work with.

Your Attraction Box can be any type of container, as simple as a shoebox, or as elaborate as a treasure chest.

Each time you put something into your Attraction Box, what you are actually offering 'vibrationally' is hope, and hope is a positive vibration. Instead of throwing out the catalogues and the flyers and saying things like "I can't afford this," or "I'll never be able to have one of these," you now allow it. You do this because it's not your job to figure out where or when your desire is going to come. Just put it into your Attraction Box and leave the rest to the Law of Attraction.

Tool #9: Create a Void or Vacuum

A void or vacuum is always waiting to be filled.

As an example let's say you're looking for more clients. By making space in your filing cabinet for new clients, even by labelling some empty file folders with the words "Next new client," it does two things – it sets the intention that you want to attract new clients and it also creates a void to be filled. Saying "I'm waiting for new clients," or "I have only a few clients," can be rephrased as "I have room and space for new clientele." Do you hear how optimistic that sounds? Does it feel better?

Some voids can be created intentionally. For example, go to your daytimer and enter this on your calendar, "New client here," or "New appointment goes here," or "Sales happen here." Now you've created the void and intention to attract those things. When you look at your calendar you'll be reminded of your intention of what you want to attract in those time slots, thus giving it more attention, energy and focus.

The other kind of void is unintentional. It's when a client cancels. When a client cancels, most people will complain or worry about the cancellation, spending too much time focusing on the cancellation and giving it negative attention. You can change the vibration by saying "I've just created a void to attract a new client," or "I've just created some more room for another project in my business."

Now, that's Allowing!

Tool #10: Allow the Law of Attraction to Figure It Out

Sometimes it can get a little overwhelming thinking about your desire and all that you need to do to obtain it. You needn't be overwhelmed because the Law of Attraction will bring the results to you.

At the very moment that you catch yourself saying:

- ◆ I don't know how to figure this out.
- ◆ I don't know where to look.
- ◆ I don't know how to find this information.
- ◆ I don't know what to do next.
- ◆ I'm having problems finding this.
- ◆ I can't figure it out.

Stop! Say to yourself "That's not my job. I'm going to allow the Law of Attraction to figure this out."

This lesson was a valuable one for my client and friend Andria. When she was first going into business for herself, she used the Law of Attraction to attract her ideal business. Using the 3-step process, Andria discovered a business that really got her excited by allowing her to shop every day. She also used the Law of Attraction to find financing and the perfect location for her clothing consignment store. Every step of the way, whenever any tough questions came up and Andria would worry about the details, I would say to her "That's not your job. Let the Law of Attraction figure it out."

Although the Law of Attraction took care of the big questions, Andria still had to do the follow-up actions. For example, after she found the name of the perfect banker, she still had to make an appointment to see him and arrange financing for her shop.

There comes a time when you need to take action. As you let the Law of Attraction figure it out and you start to receive things that are in alignment with your desire, you can then decide when to take action.

Your job is not to try to figure things out intellectually but to let the Law of Attraction figure it out.

Wrapping Up Step 3: Allowing

You have completed the 3rd step of Deliberate Attraction –
Allowing.

Here's what we've covered in this section

♦ Allowing – the 3rd step of the Deliberate Attraction
process is the most important step
♦ Allowing is the absence of doubt
♦ Doubt is a negative vibration
♦ The negative vibration of doubt cancels
the positive vibration of a desire
♦ A limiting belief is a repetitive thought
♦ When you say " I can't because…," you've just uncovered
a limiting belief
♦ Finding proof helps you remove doubt
♦ Finding evidence that others are having or doing what
you want to have or do helps remove your doubt
♦ The purpose of Allowing tools is to help you remove
doubt
♦ **10 Allowing Tools:**
- Celebrate the Evidence of Proof
- Record Proof of the Law of Attraction
- Appreciation and Gratitude
- Use the Expression, "I'm in the Process of…"
- Use the Expression, "I've Decided…"
- Use the Expression, "Lots Can Happen…"
- Ask for Information
- Make Yourself an Attraction Box
- Create a Void or Vacuum
- Allow the Law of Attraction to Figure It Out

Putting It All Together

Now that you've learned how to use the Law of Attraction to get more of what you want and less of what you don't want, you can start using the tools from this book right away.

The worksheets for Step 1, 2 and 3 plus bonus worksheets are available online for free.

Visit: www.LawofAttractionBook.com/worksheets.html

Beyond the 3-Step Formula

- **Become More Abundant and Attract More Money**

- **Relationships and Your Vibration**

- **Parents and Teachers: Learn How to Teach Law of Attraction to Children**

Abundance is a feeling. Be more deliberate to include the feeling of abundance in your current vibration – your Vibrational Bubble.

Become More Abundant and Attract More Money

You have learned so far that all feelings give off vibrations, either positive or negative. Abundance is a feeling and that's GOOD news. Why? All feelings can be duplicated! Abundance is a feeling and that feeling has a corresponding vibration that you can duplicate. In many cases people are duplicating the feeling of lack, sadness or hopelessness simply by the thoughts and the words they use. Given that you can generate feelings by your words and thoughts, you can learn how to duplicate the feelings of abundance more intentionally by changing the way you use your words and thoughts.

Law of Attraction doesn't know if you are generating a thought by remembering, pretending, creating, visualizing or daydreaming. It simply responds to our vibration in that moment, and we can only send out one vibration at a time! By creating the vibration of abundance more deliberately and more often, we are including it in our Vibrational Bubble more often, thus increasing abundance in our life.

Your objective is to include the vibration of abundance in your Vibrational Bubble as often and as long as possible. The good news is it is easy to duplicate the vibration of abundance. You may be abundant in your life every day and haven't noticed it, celebrated it, or talked about it, therefore not including it in your Vibrational Bubble.

Build a list of all the sources and resources where money and abundance can come from. Most people when asked "How could you get more money?" answer by saying that they could work more hours to earn more money, or get a part-time job to earn more money. For these people, their belief that this is the only way to increase their abundance is a limiting belief. There are actually many, many other ways where abundance is evident in your life.

On the following page there is a partial list of areas that can be deemed as abundant. In other words, when you experience anything on the following list, for most people it generates that feeling of abundance within them.

You may also notice that in many cases the feeling of abundance is not always related to money.

Sources of Abundance (examples)

- Someone treats you to lunch (or breakfast or dinner)
- Someone gives you free advice or coaching
- You receive gifts
- You receive free transportation or lodging
- You get your 2nd cup of coffee free
- Someone gives you a prize
- You buy something at a discount or on sale
- You get to use air mile points
- You win door prizes
- You trade or exchange with somebody
- You sell your products or services
- (Add more of your own...)

Other Sources of Abundance

_____

_____

_____

_____

_____

_____

_____

_____

_____

_____

_____

_____

_____

Tools for Including the Vibration of Abundance in Your Vibrational Bubble

Tool #1: Record Evidence of Your *Abundant-ness*

Keep a daily log of all the sources from which you are receiving abundance. This will significantly help you in noticing abundance in your life. Keeping a daily log shows you concrete proof (evidence) that abundance DOES exist and IS already present in your life. Celebrate! When you notice abundance, celebrate the evidence of it in your life – and while celebrating, know that you are offering the positive vibration of abundance. Remember – at every moment, including right now, the Law of Attraction is responding to the vibration you are offering and giving you more of the same. Keeping this log encourages you to spend more time celebrating your *abundant-ness*, thereby including it in your Vibration Bubble more frequently.

Here is an example of an entry in a Daily Log to track *Abundant-ness*.

I'm Abundant. Today I attracted abundance when:

◆ A friend paid for my lunch.
◆ During lunch I received a half hour of free coaching.
◆ I had free transportation to and from the airport.
◆ I received a check from a client.
◆ I received a thank-you email.
◆ I got a deal on my new eyeglasses.
◆ Others ...

Maintain your own daily log. Do this exercise for the next seven days and you will notice yourself saying "I'm so abundant! I've attracted evidence of abundance every day for the last seven days," or "I'm so abundant! I've attracted 100s of dollars of free advice in the last seven days." Ideally, you would continue to do this well beyond seven days.

Become more deliberate in your offering of the vibration of abundance and the Law of Attraction will bring you more of the same.

Use the worksheet on the next page to start logging your evidence of abundance today.

Evidence of Abundance Journal

I'm Abundant. Today I attracted...	Date:

I'm Abundant. Today I attracted...	Date:

I'm Abundant. Today I attracted...	Date:

I'm Abundant. Today I attracted...	Date:

For more copies of this worksheet, go to
www.LawofAttractionBook.com/worksheets.html

Tool #2: Always Say Yes to Money

A lot of people feel challenged to say *yes* when someone offers to pay for their lunch or buy them a gift or wants to simply give them money. Many people when offered to have their lunch paid for respond with "No that's okay, you don't need to do that," or "Oh no, I'll pay for my own. You don't have to buy me lunch," or "Oh no, I couldn't!" Does this sound like you or someone you know?

In all of these statements you can hear resistance to receiving money. The new you, however, will learn to say "Thanks, I would like that," and you'll start to feel good about it. You may experience discomfort at first but as you continue to say *yes*, it will get easier and you will feel your resistance fading away. This in turn opens up your allowing for more money. Start saying yes to money today!

Tool #3: Hold Onto That Check

Do you want to raise your vibration when it comes to receiving more money? Then hang onto checks you've received for a little bit longer.

Instead of cashing a check the day you get it, holding onto it will generate more 'vibrational' value if you observe it for a day or more. Every time you view the check you will get a little jolt of excitement that will be offered to the Law of Attraction.

Remember that each time you feel that little jolt of excitement, you are now including that vibration in your Vibrational Bubble. When you notice that something made you excited about money, do it over and over again. The Law of Attraction is always responding.

Wrapping Up: Abundance and Attracting More Money

Here's what we've covered in this section

◆ Be more deliberate to include the feeling of abundance in your current vibration

◆ Become aware of many different sources of abundance

◆ Recording evidence of abundance increases your attention to the vibration of abundance

◆ Your job is to include the vibration of abundance as often as possible in your Vibrational Bubble

◆ Celebrate the moment you notice you've attracted something abundant

◆ **Three tools to help you attract abundance more deliberately:**
  - Record evidence of your abundant-ness
  - Always say yes to money
  - Hold onto that check

Relationships and Your Vibration

Have you noticed at times when you meet somebody that within seconds you are saying to yourself "I don't like their energy?" At other times, you meet someone and can tell you are hitting it off with them within seconds because you catch yourself saying "I sure like their energy." These kinds of experiences show that you've already been *picking up* other peoples' energy, or vibes.

If we were to measure your vibration on a scale of 1-100, 100 being a very high vibe and 1 being a very low vibe, where would your vibe be?

Imagine a radio dial showing station '0' to station '100'. All the radio stations between 0 to 50 are negative talk-radio and all the stations from 50 to 100 are positive-talk radio.

Your vibes are similar to the vibes of radio frequencies. When you are feeling really good and everything is working out in your life, things come to you easily, and everyone in your life is positive. We could say that your vibe is as high as 98.5 on the radio dial.

How can you tell when you are on 98.5? You can tell by how you feel. You can see by the diagram and by how you are feeling when your vibe is high, that it means there is little to no negative vibration around you. When there is little to no negative vibration around you then everything comes to you much quicker. You start attracting relationships that are of a similar vibration. Some of you may also notice that as you've been moving up the dial (raising your vibration), you start attracting like-minded and like-vibration people in all areas of your life.

The distance between your vibration and someone else's vibration is equal to the amount of resistance (negativity) you feel when you are with them.

On the other hand, many of you may also be familiar with the saying "Negativity breeds negativity." Most of us have people in our lives that aren't on station 98.5 at the same time when we are. Recall a time in your life when your vibration was high. You're having one great experience followed by another and you love everything in your life. Then your telephone rings. You look at the call display and it's somebody in your life that's at a much lower vibration than you. As a matter of fact just seeing their name lowers your vibration. Let's call this person your *Negative-Nelly.*

Your *Negative-Nelly*

Some people may ask "How can I even attract a *Negative-Nelly* if I have such a high vibration?" The answer is simple. You didn't necessarily attract them by choice. The *Negative-Nelly* in your life could be, for example, your partner, workmate, colleague, child, parent or neighbor.

Let's say for example that *Negative-Nelly's* vibration is consistently low, on station 30.1, and your vibration is on 98.5. Looking at the radio station below you can see the amount of distance between your vibration and *Negative-Nelly's* vibration. The amount of distance between your vibration and someone else's vibration is equal to the amount of resistance (negativity) you feel when you are with them (or talk to them).

In the past you may have said "Hey, *Negative-Nelly* brings me down." The truth is *Negative-Nelly* didn't bring you down. You lowered your dial (vibration) to match theirs.

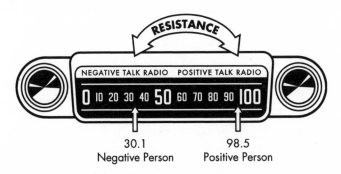

30.1
Negative Person

98.5
Positive Person

How to HOLD Your Positive Vibration

What can you do in the future to maintain your vibration at 98.5 when you are talking to people who are at a much lower vibration? Just like you can select a station (or vibration) on your car radio, you can also have a high vibration and stay there, despite having *Negative-Nelly* in your life. Here's how to do that.

The next time your *Negative-Nelly* calls you and starts to talk about how sad their life is, or how they don't like their job, don't have enough money or a satisfying relationship, you have two choices:

Choice #1: You can buy into that conversation which then lowers your vibration to match theirs… or

Choice #2: When you hear them say what they don't want, you can simply ask them "So, what do you want?"

Remember that as a *Negative-Nelly* goes from what they don't want to what they do want, their words change, and when their words change, their vibration changes so they now offer a new higher vibration. As their vibration rises it gets closer to matching yours, and the closer their vibration is to yours, the more harmonious your vibrations become.

Now you understand that when you meet somebody and you hit it off with them, saying to yourself "Did I ever click with them. Our chemistry was so good," you really mean that your vibrations are in harmony. When you meet somebody and before you even learn their name, you catch yourself saying "Wow, I don't like their energy. They're not my type," it's an indicator that your vibrations are not in harmony.

Your job is to look after your vibration and steer any conversations that you have with people to be more uplifting and positive. You do that by remembering to gently ask the question "So, what do you want?," thus helping the other person achieve a more positive and therefore higher vibration.

Attracting Your Ideal Relationship

I'll use the word 'relationship' here to indicate many kinds of relationships – perhaps your ideal partner, business relationship, your relationship with your children, parents, neighbors, work colleagues, students or clients.

Now we'll get started by using the 3-step formula for Law of Attraction to learn how to attract your ideal relationship.

Reminder: The Contrast you've experienced in the past will be helpful for your future.

Knowing what you didn't like about a past partner or a past date is very useful to you. You can use this information to help you get clarity about the kind of partner you do want. For example, if you don't want someone who works too much, what do you want? If you don't want someone who is not adventurous, what do you want? If you don't want someone who is not interested in dancing, who is not romantic, or not a good listener etc., what do you want?

Understanding what you don't want will help you generate more clarity about what you do want and your clarity becomes your new, clear desire! The easiest way to do this is to say to yourself "So, what do I want?" It sounds simple and it is! When you change your observation from what you don't want to what you do want, the vibration changes. When you change your vibration, the results will change! Notice too, how you feel when you get clear about something. It feels good when we say "Oh! That's exactly what I'd like!" This new clarity has now become your desire and that is the first step to manifesting your ideal relationship.

If you're not truly offering a vibration of the way you want it to be, then the Law of Attraction cannot respond to it. In other words, you are saying that you want THIS kind of person but you are sending out a vibe that is different than your desire. One way to check what vibration you are sending out is to observe what you ARE receiving in your life. It's always a perfect match to whatever you are offering 'vibrationally'.

Most people while in the process of attracting their ideal relationship will often spend time noticing that they have NOT been attracting exactly what they want. That noticing is causing them to send out the vibration of lack (a negative vibration). Stop observing what you are NOT attracting and you'll stop giving it your attention, energy and focus. Your job is to look for the parts of a relationship or the characteristics of a date that ARE matching your desire list and give those your attention! Your vibration will change and the Law of Attraction will bring you more of the same!

Tips for Attracting Your Ideal Relationship

Tip #1: Don't tell anyone your date was a flop!

Don't email your friends about it! Don't talk about it with your girlfriends! Don't write about it in your journal! Remember that the Law of Attraction doesn't know if you are remembering something, complaining about it, or worrying about it. The Law of Attraction will simply bring you more of whatever it is you are focusing on!

Tip #2: Build your Contrast list

Come home from your date and build a list of all the things that you didn't like about your dating experience and convert each item of contrast on your list into another thing that you clearly want.

Tip #3: Move on if it doesn't feel right

If it didn't feel good on the first date, it usually doesn't get better, so simply move on to the next date, adding to your Clarity list each time.

Tip #4: Tell why it matches

Spend time talking about it, writing about it, and daydreaming about what IS matching. Give what you like more attention, energy and focus.

Wrapping Up: Relationships and Your Vibration

Here's what we've covered in this section

♦ At every moment you are sending a vibration, either positive or negative

♦ When your vibration is high and someone else's is lower than yours, you feel resistance (negative vibration)

♦ To help maintain a high vibration when dealing with others who have a lower vibration ask them "So, what do you want?" when they are complaining or talking about what they don't want

♦ Use the Deliberate Attraction process to attract your ideal relationship

♦ **Four tips for attracting your ideal relationship:**
  - Don't tell anyone your date was a flop
  - Build a list
  - Move on if it doesn't feel right
  - Tell why it matches

Parents and Teachers:
Learn How to Teach the
Law of Attraction to Children

Imagine having everyone in your family or classroom practicing the Law of Attraction. This section is dedicated to giving you information, tools and fun games to help you teach the message of the Law of Attraction to children in an easy way.

When teaching adults, it is common to use words like 'manifestation', 'vibrations', 'synchronicity', 'serendipity' and 'coincidence'. When teaching the Law of Attraction to children, it is important to talk to them at their level using words they can relate to.

Tip #1: Keep your words simple!

Instead of using the word vibration, use *vibes*.

Recently, when asked to speak to a group of 10-year-olds in their classroom, I decided to begin my presentation by using a word they could relate to. My question to them was "Can you give me some examples of *negative vibes*?" I used the word *vibes* in place of *vibration*. The students quickly waved their hands in the air. These are some of the examples they shared:

◆ When my Mom doesn't have her coffee, she has negative vibes.
◆ When my parents fight in the house, I can feel negative vibes.
◆ When I see a bully at school, I feel negative vibes.
◆ Being in a scary building that's dark gives me negative vibes.

Clearly these kids knew exactly what a negative *vibe* was and they agreed that being around others who had negative vibes or having a negative vibe themselves was not a great feeling to have.

Tip #2: Get children to 'buy in' or 'own' a new concept by getting them to answer questions *from their own experience.*

Next I used a picture of a light switch on the blackboard, showing the 'on' and 'off' position. 'On' meant you had a positive vibe and 'Off' meant you had switched off your positive vibe and had a negative vibe instead. After having the students agree it felt better to have a positive vibe instead of negative one, I asked them if they wanted to learn how to change their negative vibe to a positive vibe. They all excitedly said "Yes."

I asked them to write these three words down in their notebooks in big letters: **DON'T, NOT** and **NO.** I then explained that when we use these words we feel negative. I asked them to give me examples of when these words were used in their lives. You can bet they had quite a list to give me. Here are some examples:

◆ Don't be late.
◆ Don't get your clothes dirty.
◆ Do not run in the halls.
◆ Don't leave your coats on the floor.
◆ No bullying.
◆ Don't play ball in the house.
◆ Don't eat or drink near the computer.

After making a list of all the examples on the blackboard, I suggested we read them together out loud. They all agreed that just saying the list out loud did indeed feel negative. In other words, I proved the point and they agreed. In doing so, I had surfaced the problem and next I presented them with a solution.

Tip #3: Kids love a secret.

Choosing my words carefully once again, I told them I would teach them a 'secret' way to turn the light switch from the 'Off' (negative vibe) position to the 'On' (positive vibe) position. I intentionally chose the word 'secret' because I knew they would treat it as something special and really want to remember it. They loved it when I told them that this 'secret' was one that very few grown-ups knew, and that with this 'secret' they could change any negative vibe into a positive one.

The students learned that the secret to switching their vibes was to ask themselves a very simple question. Each time they heard themselves saying **don't**, **not** or **no,** they were to ask themselves "So, what do I want?" Revisiting their list of don't, not and no's, we came up with a "So, what do I want?" list. The students were eager to share their answers to this secret question.

Don't, Not and No	So, What Do I Want?
Don't be late	Arrive on time
Don't get your clothes dirty	Keep your clothes clean
Do not run in the halls	Walk in the halls
Don't leave your coats on the floor	Hang up your coats
No bullying	Play nicely
Don't play ball in the house	Play ball outside
Don't eat or drink at the computer	Eat or drink at the table

As I reviewed this list with the students, they all agreed that saying what they did want felt better than saying what they didn't want.

By applying Tips 1, 2 and 3, these students grasped the entire concept of changing their vibration from negative to positive – easily and quickly!

I knew they'd be going home eager and enthusiastic to share this message with their parents and friends. So again, I reminded them they had a secret, and in order to keep the secret special, they needed to be gentle when telling others about it. This way, the next time their parents, siblings or friends used the words **don't**, **not** and **no**, they could *gently* ask the secret question "So, what do you want?"

Positive
love, excitement,
joy, fun, safe

Negative
scared, angry, sad,
left-out, lonely

Tools for Teaching the Law of Attraction to Children

Tool #1: Magnetic Board Game

An easy game to implement within any family or small group of children is the **Don't, Not and No Magnetic Board Game.** Prepare a magnetic board (or something similar) by writing the name of each family or group member across the top. Using fun magnets, the objective of the game is to get and keep the most magnets under your name at the end of each week. Start off by giving each person five magnets. Each time a member hears anyone using the words **don't, not** and **no,** the player who used those words loses a magnet to the player who noticed. Decide on a reward for the winner at the end of the week and keep it fun. Display your magnetic board in a central location. For families, an ideal place would be near your dinner table or on your fridge door so you can refer to it often. This is a fun game so parents and teachers – you play too!

Tool #2: On-Off Light Switch Poster

This poster will be a useful visual aid for younger children. Use it to help them understand the difference between feeling negative and positive emotions or vibes. I've included the following illustration to use as a guide.

First, together with the child, build a list of words that represent negative and positive emotions. Have the child help you place these words describing positive emotions on the 'ON' side of the light switch poster. Do the same for the words describing negative emotions, placing them on the 'OFF' side. As a parent or teacher, whenever you notice a child expressing an emotion, use the poster and have them find that emotion on the 'OFF' side or 'ON' side of the light switch poster. This poster will help reinforce their understanding between positive and negative vibes. Display the poster somewhere prominent where you can refer to it often.

Tool #3: The Secret Question Reminder

The purpose of this tool is to help children remember the secret question whenever they use the words **don't, not** and **no**. Using a wide rubber band, or a medallion, have your child or student label it "Secret." Now the child can wear it as a tool to help them remember to ask themselves "So, what do I want?"

Tool #4: Family or Group Meeting

For older children and teens, a weekly meeting can be a good way to learn and share about the Law of Attraction. I've included a list of questions that you can incorporate into your meeting.

◆ Are you noticing that you are reducing the number of times you use **don't, not** and **no**?
◆ When have you caught yourself using **don't, not** and **no**?
◆ Who have you taught or shared the Law of Attraction with this week?
◆ What evidence have you noticed that you are attracting more of what you want and less of what you don't?
◆ What would you like to attract more of this week?

To continue practicing the Law of Attraction between meetings, make sure everyone has each other's permission to give support in asking "So, what do you want?" Ask permission and give permission. *"Do I have your permission to mention when I notice you using* don't, not *and* no? *I give you my permission to point out to me every time you notice I'm using them!"*

Wrapping Up: Teaching the Law of Attraction to Children

Here's what we've covered in this section

◆ Simple words like *vibe* and *secret* are powerful teaching tools

◆ Ask questions that get kids to relate to concepts from their own experience (buy-in!)

◆ Use visual aids with younger children (light switch poster)

◆ Reinforce with games and rewards

◆ Parents – be sure to participate

◆ Ask permission and give permission

◆ Keep it fun

Putting It All Together

Now that you've learned how to use the Law of Attraction to get more of what you want, and less of what you don't want, you can start using the exercises and tools from this book right away.

Remember, the worksheets for Step 1, 2 and 3 plus bonus worksheets are available online for free.

Visit: www.LawofAttractionBook.com/worksheets.html

Refer to this book often for guidance. You can also make use of other resources such as articles, TeleClasses, seminars, my monthly e-zine, and my website: www.LawofAttractionBook.com

You now have the tools to let the Law of Attraction improve your life. I wish you pure joy.

Michael

Staying Connected to the Message of the Law of Attraction

Support and Resources

◆ Surrounding yourself with others who practice the Law of Attraction will help you to consistently offer a positive vibration, but how do you go about finding these people? One way is to use the Deliberate Attraction process. Use the power of the Law of Attraction to bring like-minded people into your life.

◆ Start a Law of Attraction group in your city. Find out more at www.lawofattractionbook.com/LOAdiscussiongroup.htm On this page you'll find information on how to host your own Law of Attraction discussion group.

◆ Read other books dedicated to the Law of Attraction. You'll find a list at: www.LawofAttractionBook.com/resources.html

References and Suggested Reading

Atkinson, William Walter (first edition 1906)
Thought Vibration or the Law of Attraction in the Thought World
Kessinger Publishing Company, 1998

Hanson, Rebecca *Law of Attraction for Business*
Rebecca Hanson Publisher, 2004

Hicks, Jerry and Esther *Ask and It Is Given, Learning to Manifest Your Desire (The Teachings of Abraham)*
Hay House Inc., 2005

Hill, Napoleon (first edition 1937) *Think and Grow Rich*
Renaissance Books, 2001

Holliwell, Dr. Raymond *Working with the Law*
DeVorss & Company, 2005

Holmes, Ernest (1926) (revised edition 1938)
Basic Ideas of Science of Mind
DeVorss & Company, 1957

Murphy, Dr. Joseph *The Power of the Subconscious Mind*
Reward/Prentice Hall, 1963

Peale, Norman Vincent *The Power of Positive Thinking*
Ballantine Books, 1952

Ponder, Catherine *Dynamic Law of Prosperity*
DeVorss & Company, 1985

Tracy, Brian *Universal Law of Success and Achievement*
Nightingale-Conant Corporation, 1991

Wattles, Wallace *The Science of Getting Rich*
Top of the Mountain Publishing, 1910

Special Appreciation

I was highly motivated and inspired by the works of Esther and Jerry Hicks of Abraham-Hicks Publications. It is with deep appreciation that I thank them for sharing their knowledge of the Law of Attraction with the world and with me. My life is fuller and richer because of it.

For more information about Abraham-Hicks Publications visit: www.abraham-hicks.com or call 830-755-2299.

I owe a heartfelt and much deserved thank-you to the tens of thousands of people who have attended all of my seminars and TeleClasses; the multitude of e-mails I've received telling me of your personal success stories; the hundreds of people who have called in to speak to me during my many radio talk show broadcasts – YOU are what makes MY Law of Attraction work!

Also, to all of the people who have been there with me since the beginning, supporting me physically, emotionally and spiritually – my love to you always.

About the Author

Michael Losier writes and teaches about a subject he knows very well. Over the years, Michael Losier has done a complete overhaul of his life. Although he is quick to point out that he's always had a happy life, including an untroubled childhood and a supportive family, Michael clearly states that his discovery and application of the Law of Attraction is responsible for the new level of success and fulfillment he enjoys as an author, trainer and entrepreneur.

Michael Losier grew up in a blue-collar community in New Brunswick, Canada. A student of NLP (Neuro-Linguistic Programming, a technology of psychological and behavioral modification), Losier and four other NLP students in Victoria, BC produced a successful series of annual holistic health expos beginning in 1990. In the mid-90s, Losier participated in programs that trained him as an "Empowerment Coach," and in 1995 he became a certified NLP practitioner. He then shortened his work week with the government to four days, and spent his fifth weekday coaching clients.

In 1995, Losier was introduced to the subject of Law of Attraction. This led him to wonder why he ever attracted anything negative to his life. Michael then explored Huna (the Hawaiian metaphysical system), Feng Shui and other energy-based subjects. He concluded that any topic needed to be taught in a model that people could easily embrace. "It had to be made user-friendly," he recalls.

In 1996, Michael began weekly meetings with one other Law of Attraction enthusiast. This quickly grew to a roster of 45 people meeting every two weeks. He then created Teleclass International Inc., with a business partner. TeleClasses are live, interactive training classes conducted over the telephone using state-of-the-art teleconferencing bridge systems. Losier has reached over 15,000 people a year via TeleClasses.

Michael Losier is a passionate, committed man. He is a faculty member of the Law of Attraction Training Center which trains students to become Law of Attraction Certified Practitioners.

Michael logs hundreds of hours a year as a radio and TV talk-show guest and is also a frequent keynote speaker/trainer at Positive Living Centers, spiritual centers, businesses, corporations and conventions in the U.S., Canada and Mexico.

When Michael gets his way – and he often does when it comes to spreading the message of Law of Attraction – millions will soon be using his powerful system to improve their lives. This will be a true win-win outcome for all concerned.

When Michael isn't teaching, leading or learning, he enjoys hiking through old-growth forests of the Pacific Northwest and tending to his patio garden in Victoria, B.C., Canada.